START-UP
HISTORY

Remembrance Day

Jane Bingham & Ruth Nason

W

Franklin Watts

Copyright © White-Thomson Publishing 2016

All rights reserved.

ISBN 978 1 4451 3491 8

A CIP catalogue record for this book is
available from the British Library.

Editor: Ruth Nason
Designer: Helen Nelson, Jet the Dog
Consultants: Sandra Bird, Headteacher, The Grove Infant and Nursery School, Harpenden;
Dr Anne Punter, Partnership Tutor, School of Education, University of Hertfordshire.
Packaged by: White-Thomson Publishing www.wtpub.co.uk

This book was first published by Evans Brothers Ltd. It has been revised and fully updated in line with the KS1 History curriculum.

Picture credits
Key: t=top, b=bottom, l=left, r=right

Cover: Paul Brown/Alamy Stock Photo, Paul Popper/Popperfoto; p1 Thinkstock; p4 t Thinkstock/Chris Jackson, p4 b Topfoto; p5 t Royal British Legion, p5 b Thinkstock; p6 Michael Nason, p7 Michael Nason, p8 Shutterstock/Monkey Business Images; p9 t Hulton-Deutsch Collection/Corbis; p9 b Hulton-Deutsch Collection/Corbis; p10 Paul Popper/Popperfoto; p11 t Hulton-Deutsch Collection/Corbis; p11 b Popperfoto/Getty Images; p12 Popperfoto/Getty Images; p13 Bob Thomas/Popperfoto/Getty Images; p14 Thinkstock/claudiodivizia; p15 t Bettmann/Corbis; p15 b Hulton-Deutsch Collection/Corbis; p16 Topham Picturepoint; p17 Thinkstock/Digoarpi; p18 Corbis; p19 Thinkstock/Pawelkowalczyk; p20 Thinkstock/Canadapanda; p21 l Dreamstime/Anizza; p21 tr Tim Graham/Getty; p21 br Dreamstime/Anita Patterson Peppers.

Printed in China

Franklin Watts
An imprint of
Hachette Children's Group
Part of The Watts Publishing Group
Carmelite House
50 Victoria Embankment
London EC4Y 0DZ

An Hachette UK Company
www.hachette.co.uk

www.franklinwatts.co.uk

MIX
Paper from
responsible sources
FSC® C104740

Every effort has been made by the Publishers to ensure that the websites in this book are suitable for children, and that they contain no inappropriate or offensive material. However, because of the nature of the Internet, it is impossible to guarantee that the contents of these sites will not be altered. We strongly advise that Internet access is supervised by a responsible adult.

Contents

What is Remembrance Day?

Remembrance **Day is a special day in November.**

◄ **What do you notice about these people on Remembrance Day?**

Remembrance   **November**

Remembrance means remembering. On Remembrance Day we remember people who have suffered and died in wars.

▶What feelings do you have when you remember people in wars?

▲Look at the poppies that the people are wearing.

Later in this book you will find out why poppies show remembrance for people who died in wars.

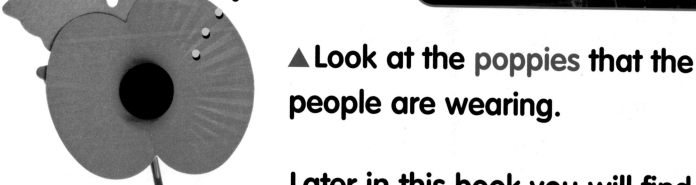

suffered   wars   poppies

People who died

One way to find out about people who died in wars is to visit a **war memorial**.

▼ Which two wars are named on this memorial?

war memorial

▶ There are names around the bottom of this war memorial.

The names are men who went to fight for Britain in the world wars. They died in the fighting.

Why do you think that some of the surnames are the same?

fight   world wars

The world wars

Think about families, to help you understand when the two world wars happened.

◄ **Do you have photographs of you** and your family?

Are there old photographs of your parents, grandparents and even great-grandparents?

photographs

▶ Was someone in your family a child at the time of the Second World War, like this?

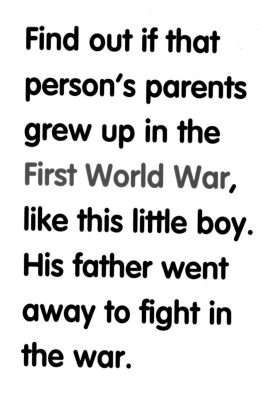

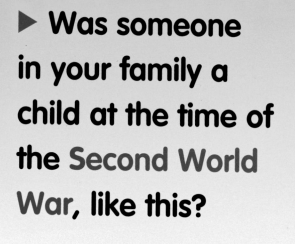

Find out if that person's parents grew up in the First World War, like this little boy. His father went away to fight in the war.

Second World War   **First World War**   **9**

The First World War

The First World War began in 1914. Millions of men joined the army which went to fight in the war. What do you think it was like for them?

army   nurses

▶ Nurses went to the battlefields to care for soldiers who were injured. Many soldiers and nurses were killed in the war.

◀ Many buildings were destroyed in the fighting. What do you think happened to the people in this village?

battlefields   **injured**   **destroyed** 11

The end of the war

The First World War was between countries all over the world. It was called the Great War because it was so big.

▶ After four years, the leaders of the countries agreed to stop the fighting. Here they are after they signed the ceasefire agreement.

Great War　　**leaders**　　**signed**

The ceasefire was at 11 o'clock in the morning on 11th November 1918. Count on from the first month of the year. Which number month is November?

▼ Later on, people held street parties to celebrate the end of the war.

ceasefire   agreement   celebrate **13**

Ways to remember

After the war, people wanted to do something special to remember all the men who had died.

War memorials were built, like the one on page 6.

◄ This war memorial in London is called the Cenotaph. (Say sen-oh-taf.)

Cenotaph   Armistice

► 11th November was called Armistice Day. People began to hold ceremonies of remembrance on this day.

◄ On Armistice Day, many people stood silent for two minutes to remember. Why do you think the silence started at 11 o'clock?

ceremonies   silent   **15**

Why poppies?

Soldiers who have been in a war are called veterans. After the First World War, some veterans made paper poppies for Armistice Day.

◄ These veterans made poppy wreaths.

The poppies were sold and the money was used to help veterans.

veterans   wreaths

The paper poppies were like the real poppies that grew in the battlefields of the First World War.

▶ Real poppies are a beautiful bright red, but soon they die.

Why do you think poppies are a good symbol of soldiers who died in the battlefields?

symbol

More wars

People hoped that war would never happen again, but then there was a Second World War. Many smaller wars still happen today.

▶ In the Second World War, planes dropped bombs on towns and cities.

bombs

After the Second World War, more names were added to war memorials. People held a ceremony of remembrance every November.

Now the ceremonies are on the second Sunday in November. This is called Remembrance Day.

◀ Veterans still make and sell poppies for Remembrance Day. The poppies help us to remember people who died in the world wars and in other wars.

Remembering today

▼ **Every Remembrance Day people go to a ceremony at their war memorial.**

Which people in uniform can you see?

uniform

► In London the Queen lays a poppy wreath at the Cenotaph.

▼ Veterans take part in parades.

► People wear poppies. At 11 o'clock they stay silent for two minutes to remember.

Why do you think it is important to remember together at the same time?

Further information for

New history words and words about Remembrance Day highlighted in the text:

agreement	celebrate	Great War	photographs	signed	war memorial
Armistice	Cenotaph	injured	poppies	silent	wars
army	ceremonies	leaders	Queen	suffered	world wars
battlefields	destroyed	November	Remembrance	symbol	wreaths
bombs	fight	nurses	Second World	uniform	
ceasefire	First World War	parades	War	veterans	

Background Information

Remembrance Day is observed in the UK, the Commonwealth nations and in some European countries, including France and Belgium. It is a day of remembrance, commemorating the men and women killed in both world wars and in later conflicts.

The first Remembrance ceremony was held in London on 11 November 1919. At 11 a.m. people stopped in the street and most of the traffic in the city came to a halt. The service was held at the grave of an unknown soldier from the First World War, and a temporary Cenotaph was built from wood to mark the grave. The current Cenotaph was built between 1919 and 1920 and poppies were first sold to the British public in 1921. The paper poppies are made by war veterans at the Royal British Legion factory in Richmond, Surrey. Money raised from the sale of poppies goes to support injured and retired war veterans and their dependants.

In the UK, Remembrance Day ceremonies are now held on the second Sunday in November. The ceremony in London is always attended by the Queen or a leading member of the royal family and by members of the British government. All the armed services (army, air force, navy and marines) are represented. There are also representatives from all the major world religions.

THE FIRST WORLD WAR (1914-18)

The First World War was fought between the Central European Powers (led by Germany and Austria-Hungary) and the Allies (Britain, France and Russia and the members of the British Empire). The USA joined the war on the Allies' side in 1917. By the end of the conflict, an estimated 10 million people had been killed and twice that number wounded. The war was fought in northern France and Belgium, in the Middle East, in Africa, in the air and at sea. Sometimes known as the 'Great War', it was thought at the time to be 'the war to end all wars'.

THE SECOND WORLD WAR (1939-45)

The Second World War involved over 60 nations, and fighting took place on the continents of Africa, Asia and Europe, as well as in the air and at sea. Altogether, 70 million people served in the armed forces during the war and 17 million service people died.

OTHER WARS

Since the Second World War, British troops have fought in Korea, in the Falkland Islands and in the Arabian Gulf. More recently, they have been involved in conflicts in Kosovo, Afghanistan and Iraq. The British services have also provided peacekeeping units in many troubled areas of the world.

Parents and Teachers

Suggested Activities

Explore the children's experiences of remembering. Which sad and serious things do they sometimes remember? It is likely that someone will remember a pet that died. If the children think of an animal or person who has died, talk about the good things about them that they remember, rather than about the sadness of the loss. Think about how we can 'capture' special things or people that we want to remember (e.g. photographs, keeping objects associated with them, anniversaries). The children may like to bring photos and objects that help them to remember something or someone. What is it about certain people and events that makes us want to remember them? A good story to read in the context of these discussions is *Badger's Parting Gifts* by Susan Varley (Andersen, 2013).

Visit a local war memorial. What can we learn about the people who died? (How old were they when they died? How many came from the same family?) How could we find out more? Invite the children to show any family photographs or memorabilia from the two world wars. Perhaps a family member could come to talk to the class about their memories of wartime. Help the children to appreciate that ordinary everyday life goes on during wartime. Focus on what children's experience would have been.

Children may have experience of a local Remembrance Day ceremony, e.g. as part of a uniformed organisation. You could also watch a video recording of some of the Remembrance Day ceremony in London. Let the children appreciate that many people are taking part in the commemoration at the same time.

After talking with the children about what we are remembering, give them some quiet time to reflect.

'Red Nose Day' is a useful reference to explain how a simple symbol represents something serious that we think about.

Further Information

BOOKS

FOR CHILDREN

Charlie's War Illustrated – Remembering World War One, by Mick Manning and Brita Granström (Franklin Watts, 2014)

Dear Jelly: Family Letters from the First World War, by Sarah Ridley (Franklin Watts, 2014)

Great Events: Remembrance Day, by Gillian Clements (Franklin Watts, 2014)

My Uncle's Dunkirk, by Mick Manning and Brita Granström (Franklin Watts, 2011)

FOR ADULTS

The Soldier's War: The Great War Through Veterans' Eyes, Richard van Emden, Bloomsbury, 2009

Eyewitness: World War I and Eyewitness: World War II, Dorling Kindersley, 2011 and 2012

WEBSITES

A quiz about Remembrance Day:
www.bbc.co.uk/newsround/13847223

Colouring sheets that can be downloaded and printed:
www.britishlegion.org.uk/media/3084682/ColouringSheet_Poppies.pdf

PLACES TO VISIT

The Imperial War Museum in London, Duxford (Cambridgeshire) and Manchester
The Royal British Legion Poppy Factory, Richmond, Surrey
The Cenotaph, London, and local war memorials

Index